ROMA
ON THE
WIGHT

The Coming of the Romans

Background to the Roman Conquest

Early in the 1st Century BC the main trading route between Britain and the rest of Europe was through the tribal regions of Brittany and Dorset. Hengistbury Head was an important port, and the Isle of Wight was well placed to benefit from passing trade. Julius Caesar's

conquest of France and south east England in the mid 1st century BC ended this situation. New political and trading relations were started between the Roman Empire and the tribes of the south east. At this time the Greek writer Strabo listed the main exports from Britain as: corn, cattle, gold, silver, iron, hides, slaves and hunting dogs.

At the start of the 1st century AD there were two tribal groups across the Solent from the Isle of Wight. To the east of the river Avon were the Atrebates, a Belgic people from north west France. They had close ties with the Roman Empire. West of the Avon however, the Durotriges of Dorset were hostile to the growing influence of Rome in the area. They were not Belgic and, as their powerful hillfort towns show, they were fiercely independent. Both tribes were successful farming and trading communities who used coins in their business dealings. Late Iron Age coins found on the Isle of Wight show that Islanders had contacts with the Atrebates and Durotriges. For this reason we are still unsure whether they were for or against the Roman invasion.

The Roman Conquest

There appear to be several reasons why the Romans invaded Britain in AD 43. North of the Atrebates another Belgic tribe, the Catuvellauni, had grown very powerful in southern England. In an attempt to gain more control over the Atrebates they seem to have supported a revolt. As a result Verica, the Attrebatic king, was driven out by the anti-Roman party and fled to Rome. There he sought the help of Claudius who had recently been made Emperor by the army. For this reason Claudius needed a military victory to impress the Roman people, and keep the legions happy. South east Britain was an attractive target. It had good agricultural land

opposite: *Map of Southern England before the conquest.*

Iron Age staters found on the Island from Brittany, the Atrebates and the Durotriges.

this page: *Bust of Emperor Claudius.*
Legionary. 1st Cent. AD.

Sestertius of Emperor Vespasian AD 69-79

and valuable metal resources, such as iron, gold, silver and lead. In fact one of the early actions after the conquest was to place all mining operations under Imperial control.

We do not know how Islanders reacted to the invasion. A clue is provided by the Roman writer Suetonius in his biography of the future Emperor Vespasian. In it he tells us that Vespasian fought 30 battles in Britain, took control of two powerful tribes, over 20 hill forts, and the Isle of Wight. The account of this campaign might suggest that the Island was taken by force. On the other hand there is little indication of early Roman military activity, and no evidence of a Roman fort. Perhaps then the Island was pro-Roman and Suetonius included it in his list to enhance Vespasian's image.

Before and after the Roman Conquest

We would like to know much more about the Isle of Wight during the pre-Roman Iron Age than we do at present. Our evidence is drawn from aerial photographs and archaeological excavation, but more fieldwork is needed to give us a clearer picture of this period.

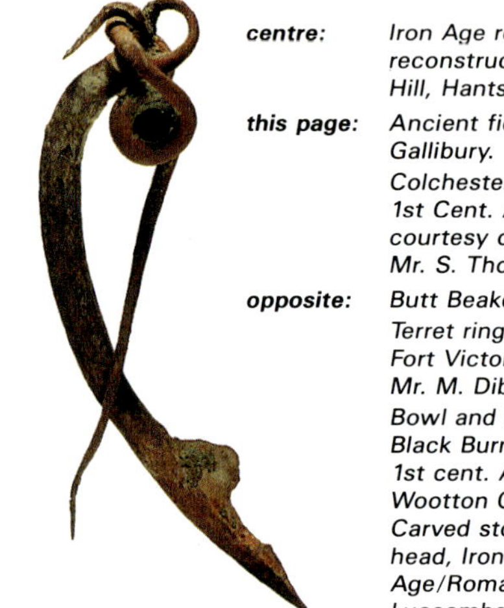

centre: *Iron Age round house reconstructed at Buster Hill, Hants.*

this page: *Ancient field system near Gallibury.*
Colchester type brooch, 1st Cent. AD, Clatterford, courtesy of Mr. S. Thompson.

opposite: *Butt Beaker.*
Terret ring, 1st cent. AD, Fort Victoria, courtesy of Mr. M. Dibelius.
Bowl and lid, Durotrigian Black Burnished Ware, 1st cent. AD, Wootton Creek.
Carved stone head, Iron Age/Roman, Luccombe.

Landscape

The study of plant pollen which survives in the soil, has shown that the Island has been farmed since the late Bronze Age. Iron Age ploughs were not good enough to break up the heavy clay soils of the north which remained

largely wooded. The trees provided materials for a wide range of household and building uses. The soils of the chalk downland and Greensand plain in the south were the best areas for farming, as they are today. By the late Iron Age agriculture on the Island was a successful mixture of cereal and animal farming. This is confirmed by the increase of grass and cereal pollen during the Iron Age detected in samples taken from sites around the Island. Aerial photographs of the chalk downs suggest the landscape was a patchwork of fields which remained much the same during the Roman period.

Settlement

The current evidence seems to show that most people lived in the southern half of the Island. Two sorts of settlement have been identified.

Open sites with round houses, such as at Sudmoor, near Brook, and enclosed settlements ringed by banks and ditches, such as at Knighton. At present there are four known areas of occupation around Newport, Brading, Knighton and in the Undercliff. The only hillfort known is at Chillerton. The size of its single rampart indicates that it was built for defence against some threat from the mainland or from the Romans.

The People

Most people in Iron Age society were peasant farmers, but there were also slaves and skilled craftsmen. These groups were ruled by the nobles, who included religious leaders and kings. However, by the time of the conquest this society had already begun to change as a consequence of two events that occurred during the 1st century BC. The first was the arrival of Belgic people from France, the second was Caesar's invasion of Southern England. The result was the development of closer political and economic ties with the Roman Empire. In the south east this led to the growth of towns as centres of trade, government and coin production. All these factors led to social unrest and fighting within tribal groups and between tribal kingdoms.

The Impact of the Conquest

To administer the new province of Britannia the country was divided into regions called *Civitates*. In southern England the old tribal kingdom of the Atrebates was divided into three civitates with centres at Silchester, Winchester and Chichester. As a reward for supporting the invasion it appears that the Romans made a local noble, Cogidubnus, ruler of this territory. They also built a splendid palace for him at Fishbourne in Sussex. Bembridge Limestone was used in the construction, and may indicate that the Isle of Wight was placed under his control.

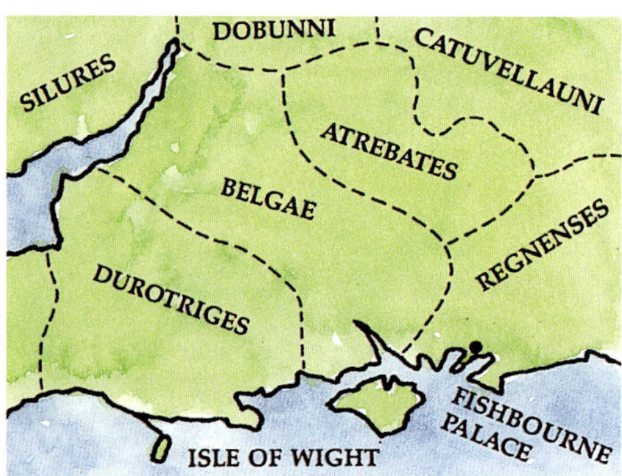

At Combley Roman villa the earliest buildings seem to be similar to granary houses at the military supply depot at the head of Chichester harbour. They are dated by pottery to the late 1st century AD, and might have been used for the collection of corn needed to supply the Roman army.

Signs of new arrangements such as this are few. The biggest impact of the Roman invasion was political and there was little change to the daily lives of ordinary Islanders. Archaeological evidence shows that they still lived in the same places, and the local pottery industry begun in the late Iron Age continued to serve local needs.

On the Island the first signs of social and economic change were the construction of villa farms at Newport, Brading and Combley, on or near to late Iron Age settlements. At present it is the villas that provide us with our evidence for the history of Roman Wight, and to which we next turn our attention.

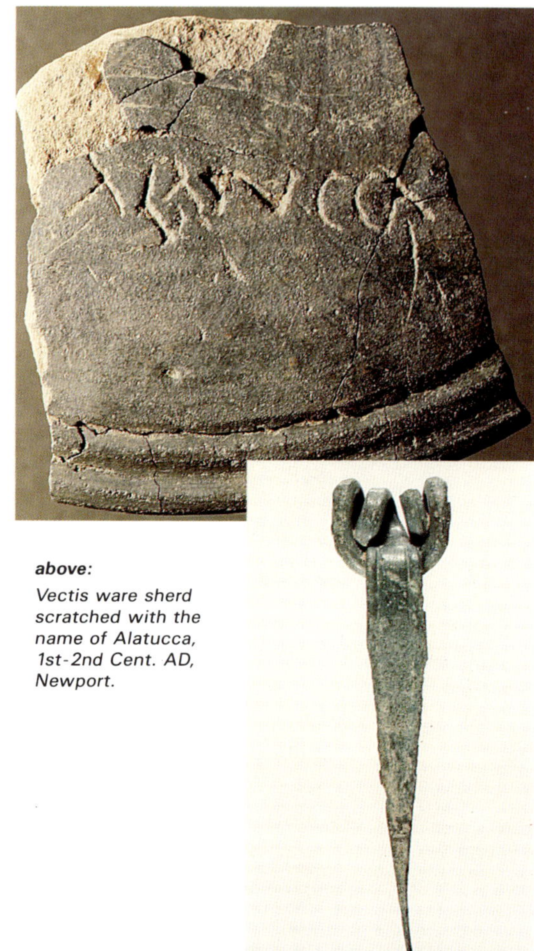

above: *Vectis ware sherd scratched with the name of Alatucca, 1st-2nd Cent. AD, Newport.*

right: *Neuheim Derivative brooch, 1st Cent. BC – 1st Cent. AD, Wroxall.*

above: *Map of Vectis (Isle of Wight) and Southern England after the Conquest.*

Roman Villas and their Construction

What is a Roman villa?

The word "villa" is the Latin term for a farm. Most of them were the country homes of wealthy Romano-British farmers. In contrast to the native round house they had rectangular ground plans. A villa also included a range of functional buildings such as barns, granaries and workshops, and an estate incorporating other settlements.

Over 700 villas have been found, mainly in Southern England, which formed the agricultural heartland of Roman Britain. They formed part of a market-orientated economy, and developed in response to the growth of new towns and the needs of the army.

Types of Villas on Roman Wight

There are four general types of villa found in Roman Britain and examples of each have been found on the Island: a cottage house at Rock; a winged-corridor house at Newport; a courtyard villa complex at Brading; and aisled farmhouses at Combley and Carisbrooke. Of the other known villas, Gurnard has been lost to the sea, and Bowcombe and Clatterford await further investigation.

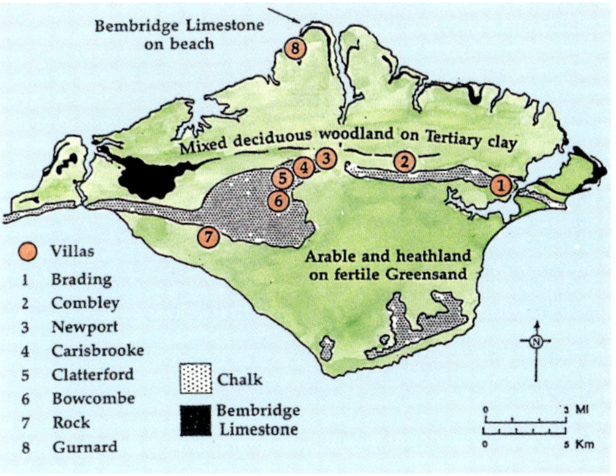

Materials

All the materials for construction could be obtained locally. Clay for bricks and tiles was widely available. Walls were made of flint gathered from arable fields, chalk and Greensand from the downs, and Bembridge Limestone from coastal outcrops. Timber for supports, floors and roofs was probably obtained from the northern woodlands.

Map showing the distribution of villas and natural resources of the Island.

below: *Plan of Gurnard Roman Villa excavated in 1866.*

Building Techniques

New methods of construction enabled villa buildings to be bigger and more complex than native structures. Solid building platforms were essential and at Combley and Rock a level base was created by cutting into the hillside. Villas had foundation trenches which were filled with flint nodules to support the stone walls. Although at Combley and Rock the builders found that additional support was needed to solve particular problems they encountered.

The walls of the villas were usually built of stone up to about one metre high. Flint and Greensand was commonly used and Bembridge Limestone was chosen because of its strength for important features, such as the corners of walls, door-ways and arches. Mortar, which was a new material, was used to bind

the walls together. It was made of sand, water and lime and when mixed with crushed brick it produced a strong waterproof concrete called *opus signinum*. This was reserved, however, for costly features such as the foundations for mosaics, or the linings of baths.

The superstructures of the villas have disappeared, but evidence suggests that on top of the dwarf stone walls a timber frame was built. The spaces are thought to have been

Nail types, Brading Villa.

left:
Bembridge Limestone roof tiles, Newport Villa.

below:
Reconstruction section of outside wall at Newport Villa showing wattle and daub.

filled with wattle and daub, which consisted of hurdles covered on both sides with a mixture of clay, dung and straw.

We do not know whether the outside walls of the buildings were left exposed, or covered with mortar. At Newport villa evidence has recently been found to suggest that it was painted red, as were some houses in the Roman town of Silchester.

Evidence from various Romano-British sites indicates that villas could have windows up to one metre square. Pale green glass found at Brading and Newport has shown that at least some windows of Island villas were glazed.

Timber was an important element in villa construction, the direct evidence for which has not survived. The stone plinths of aisled buildings show us the position of the large timber posts necessary to support these structures. Wooden joints were fastened using large nails designed to be hidden when hammered into place. Timber roofs were covered with either stone slabs or red clay

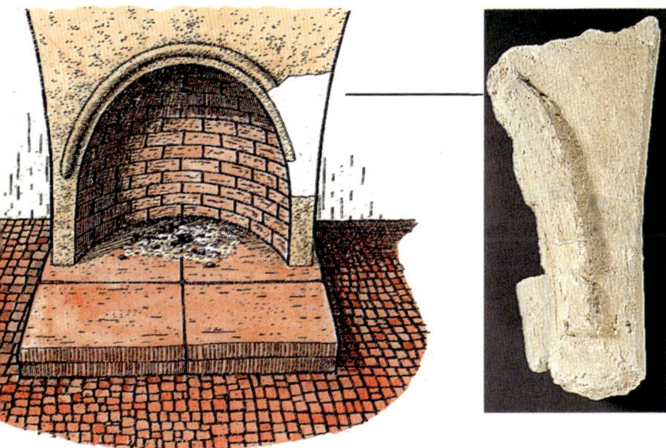

Reconstruction view of fireplace at Newport Villa showing fragment of plaster moulding.

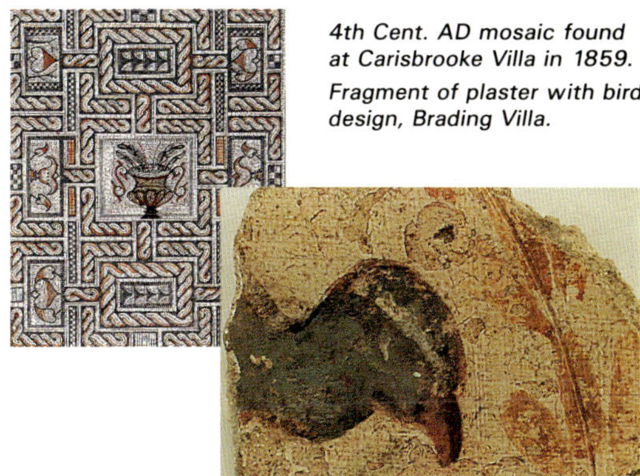

4th Cent. AD mosaic found at Carisbrooke Villa in 1859.

Fragment of plaster with bird design, Brading Villa.

tiles, and made secure using mortar and special nails. A large collection of these were found at Rock and Brading.

Internal Fixtures

Villas were heated in a number of ways, including underfloor systems called *hypocaust* and by fireplaces. The floors of the rooms were made of compacted rubble, or tessellated. The latter involved the use of stone or brick which had been cut into small square pieces called *tesserae*. Sometimes they were used together to make chequer-board or other patterns. Mosaic floors composed of different coloured tesserae were laid at Brading, Combley, Newport and Carisbrooke. Their designs and images have helped to date periods of villa building.

Mortar was plastered on the inside walls, over which bright coloured designs were painted. Most of the Island villas have produced fragments of wall paintings, but no complete examples exist. At Carisbrooke and Brading large portions were discovered still intact on the walls, but alas the excavators knew nothing of how to preserve them.

Skilled craftsmen and designers were needed to create the wall paintings and mosaics of the Island villas. For their images they used sources from throughout the Empire not just Britain.

Rock Roman Villa

This was an example of a 'cottage' type of villa, with a simple rectangular ground plan. It had five rooms which would be entered from a hall running the length of the house.

Discovery and Excavation

Rock was the first Roman villa to be discovered on the Island. The Rev. Edmund Kell informs us that around 1840 a building was found in a ploughed field east of Buddlehole spring, near Brighstone.

In 1974 it was found that the site had been badly damaged by ploughing. Further damage seemed likely so a full excavation was conducted between 1974-1976.

right: *Plan of the villa.*
below: *Interpretive view of the villa in decline.*

Rev. E. Kell.

The Building of the Villa

Coins and pottery found on the site suggest that the villa house was built between AD 275 and 300. A building platform was prepared by cutting into the hillside and then creating a hard floor of chalk sealed with mortar. The walls were built mainly of flint, and tumble from the north wall showed that they stood about 5 metres high when finished. Bembridge Limestone was used to strengthen the corners of the walls and for roofing. Many fragments of painted plaster show that some rooms were decorated. The evidence suggests that the house had a second storey, with the main living rooms upstairs. Unfortunately, later activities cleared away almost all signs of the main occupation of the villa.

Coin of Constantine I AD 318-319.
New Forest Ware flask.

The Villa in Decline

The heyday of the villa was short-lived and by about AD 330 it was already falling down. It appears that the central part of the house was taken down on purpose.

This event marks a change in the use of the building, with various farming activities now taking place. A T-shaped corn-drying oven was built at this time and the excavators found several *quern* stones used for grinding corn by hand into flour.

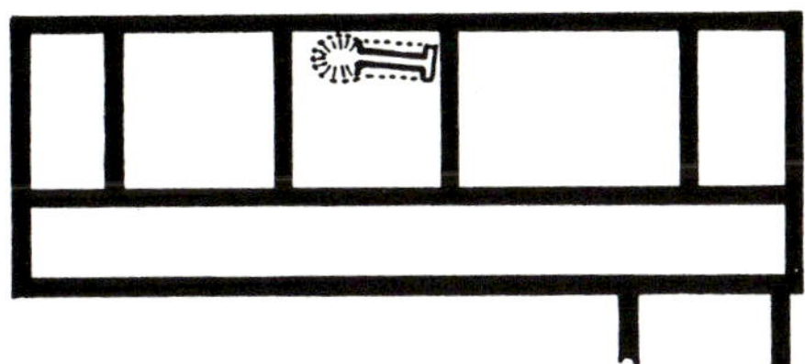

left: *Hertfordshire puddingstone quern.*

below: *Greensand Saddle quern and muller.*

The disused rooms at the west end still seem to have been roofed. A barn owl used one room to nest in, no doubt attracted by the rodents living there. A study of the owl's food remains revealed that they fell into a thick dusty type of soil common in farm buildings where cereal crops are processed and stored.

Another study has shown that animals were being slaughtered and butchered in the west end of the entrance hall. Evidence from the bones has shown that meat was being prepared for a small local community. They have also revealed that animals kept on the villa estate included sheep, cattle, pigs and horses.

The excavators found the shallow graves of two young children in the western wing. In rural areas in Roman Britain burials such as this are quite common. The cause of death is unclear: explanations offered include infanticide, disease, and ritual killing.

Destruction

Some time between AD 350 - 400 the west wall fell inwards, and the north wall collapsed on to the corn-drier. After this the ruin was seldom visited. Gradually soil built up over the site aided by farming activities.

Combley Roman Villa

The villa at this site was of a type known as an aisled farmhouse. It is believed that these buildings started as large open houses with space for people, animals and working areas. In time dividing walls were added to create living rooms, halls and other sections for farming activities.

Discovery and Excavation

Roman finds from fields near to Combley farm were first reported in 1867, but no excavation was started until 1910. In that year Arthur Arnold discovered the bath house and several

other rooms. Much to the surprise of more recent excavators Arnold seems to have put the few objects he found in a tin box and reburied them on the site. Further excavations between 1968 and 1979 were undertaken by the Isle of Wight Natural History and Archaeological Society, directed by Mr. L. R. Fennelly. These investigations uncovered a large aisled farmhouse situated on the northern slopes of the central downs.

The First Villa

Shortly after the Conquest flint-footed timber buildings were erected on the site. These continued in use into the 2nd century AD. To the north of these early structures a small cottage villa was built in the 2nd century AD. This twin-roomed house was constructed on a platform cut into the hill slope. Both of its rooms had flint floors sealed with mortar, but the eastern chamber was fitted with hypocaust heating.

The Aisled Farmhouse

Adjoining the cottage an aisled farmhouse was built in the late 2nd century AD. To take the heavy load the foundations were underpinned with oak piles and the Ironstone ground

left: *Floor tile finger-scribed with an R.*

right: *Interpretive view of the Villa in its final form.*

course was set on a bedding of flint rubble. The plan and construction of the aisled building shows that one section served as living quarters and the other was used for agricultural purposes. The apartments were

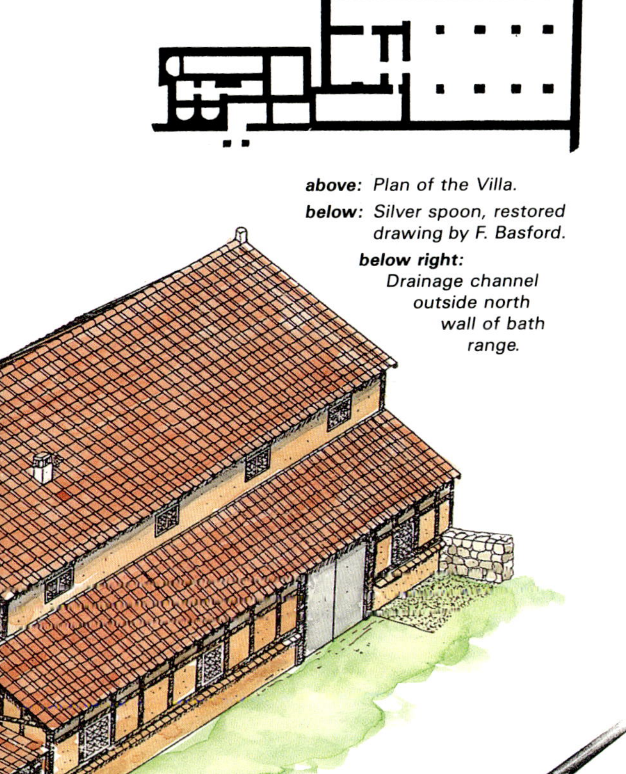

above: *Plan of the Villa.*
below: *Silver spoon, restored drawing by F. Basford.*
below right: *Drainage channel outside north wall of bath range.*

entered through a room with a geometric mosaic. Simpler tessellated floors were laid in the other three chambers. The largest of these had a fireplace and was probably the main living room. The aisled hall had two parallel rows of pier-bases made of Bembridge Limestone to carry the timber posts supporting the tiled roof. Between the piers a bedding trench suggested that dividing walls were built to create areas for different activities, such as storage, or stalling animals.

A curtain wall was also built at this time in front of the new villa to form a courtyard.

The Bath House

During the last quarter of the 3rd century AD a bath house extension was built. Unlike the other buildings the bath house had flint stone walls 3 metres high and Bembridge Limestone roof slabs. Because it was built into the hillside measures had to be taken to stop soil from sliding down-slope on to the building. Stone-lined gulleys were laid to help drainage and a timber wall was erected at the rear to hold back any earth movement.

Part of the work involved the conversion of the old cottage. Floor levels were altered and a surviving mosaic of a dolphin suggests the baths had expensive decoration. To complete the new works an entrance porch and passage-way were added giving access to the baths and living quarters.

The End of the Villa

Evidence suggests that Combley was an important centre of the local brown burnished pottery industry. Yet little pottery at all was found in layers dated to the 4th Century AD. This indicates that there was a rapid decline in the fortunes of the villa, but exactly when and why it was abandoned remains unknown. The build-up of ploughsoil over the fallen walls certainly shows that the area continued to be farmed.

Newport Roman Villa

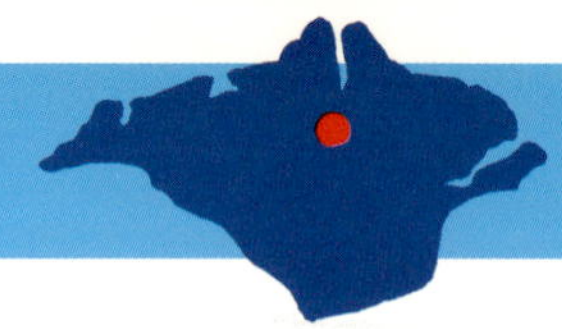

Newport was a winged-corridor type of villa. It consisted of three parts: a long rectangular house with several rooms; a projecting room on each end; and an entrance corridor in front.

Discovery and Excavation

In 1926 workmen building a garage found some Roman roof tiles and the next day they uncovered a mosaic floor. News of the discovery was reported in the Isle of Wight County Press which started a public fund to pay for an excavation. Percy Stone, a local historian and architect, directed the work under the gaze of many Islanders who came to watch the dig. By the summer of 1927 Stone had revealed the plan of the villa.

At this point Mr. Millgate, a local magistrate, bought the site and paid for a cover building to protect the remains. In 1961 the site was given to the Isle of Wight County Council. Evidence for other Roman buildings has been found nearby to show that the full story of the villa still lies buried under the neighbouring houses, gardens and streets.

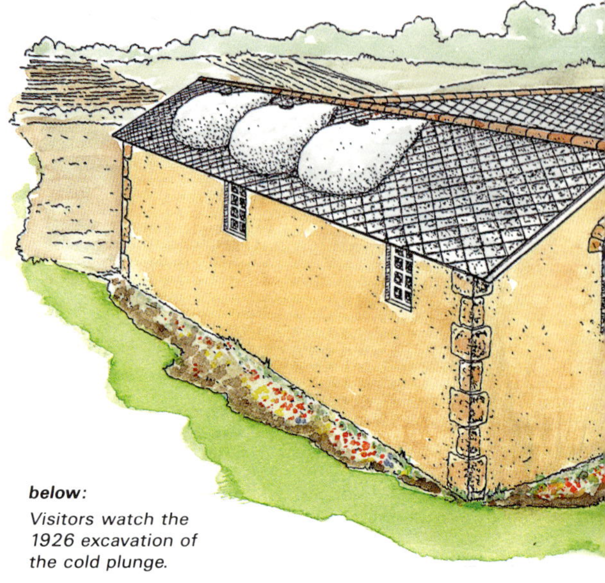

below:
Visitors watch the 1926 excavation of the cold plunge.

Early Settlement

The villa lies close to an important fording point across the River Medina. Under the villa the excavators discovered a ditch containing pottery dating from the late 1st century AD. A

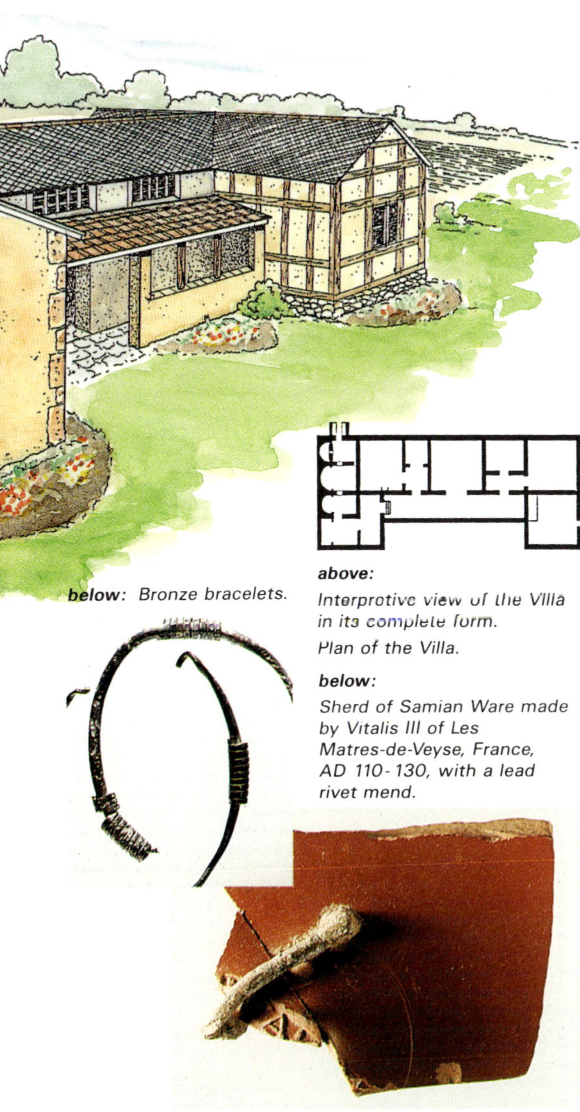

above:
Interprotive view of the Villa in its complete form.
Plan of the Villa.

below: *Bronze bracelets.*

below:
Sherd of Samian Ware made by Vitalis III of Les Matres-de-Veyse, France, AD 110-130, with a lead rivet mend.

circular depression in the corner of another room also suggests the presence of a grain storage pit or well. In 1981 further signs of activity were discovered dating from the late 1st century AD and carrying on into the 2nd century AD. The evidence included the post-holes of a building, salt-making vessels, roof tiles, and a rubbish dump with pottery and oyster shells.

left: *Woman's skull.*
below: *View of the baths showing hypocaust.*

Villa Occupation

The 1981 excavation provided new pottery evidence that the villa we know today was not built until the late 3rd century AD.

The villa seems to have been built in one operation. The whole of one end formed a superb bath range with mosaic floors, baths, and sweat rooms. The dining room had a red tessellated floor with a chequer-board design in the centre and a fireplace. The wing at the other end of the house also had a hypocaust, suggesting it was a special room.

The End of the Villa

Coin evidence indicates that during the early 4th century AD the way of life in the villa changed. The floors of the eastern rooms were taken up and one room appears to have been used as a blacksmith's workshop. How life in the villa ended is unknown. Whether the skull of a woman, aged 30-35, found in the corner of a room was the result of an attack by raiders is open to question. Perhaps it was a ritual killing, a murder, or maybe there is a less violent explanation.

Brading Roman Villa

left: *Photograph of the excavators, the man in the deerstalker may be John Price.*

Orpheus mosaic. Around the lyre-player are a fox, a monkey and two birds.

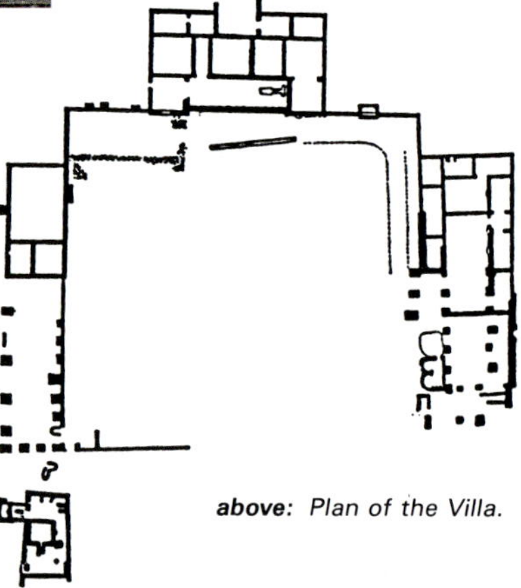

above: *Plan of the Villa.*

Brading was an example of a courtyard villa which consisted of a series of buildings around a square courtyard. These were the largest types of villa and were owned by the wealthiest Roman-Britons.

Discovery and Excavation

In 1879 a retired army Captain, John Thorp, wrote in his notebook that he had found what he suspected were Roman buildings. These structures were buried under land belonging to Morton Farm, near Brading, which local people called Stony field. Thorp had actually been searching the area for a Roman site after reading about finds discovered at Morton. The first excavations, started by accident in March 1880 when the local farmer called Munns found a mosaic whilst he was penning his sheep. He sent for Thorp and together they uncovered seven rooms of a villa house. Two London archaeologists, John Price and Hilton Price, carried on with the excavations, revealing several buildings before they finished in 1882.

Brading was poorly excavated by today's standards. The Victorian excavators had only two simple goals: to find out the plans and buildings on the site and to recover the contents of each room. Unfortunately the evidence has produced more questions than answers about the history of the villa.

The Villa Buildings

What we see today is the villa complex at its full extent dating to around AD 300. There were three main units linked by a wall to form a large inner courtyard. Facing east towards the

above:
Linchpin of 1st Cent. AD style.

below right:
The fabulous beasts in this panel are probably based on Mediterranean hunting mosaics.

below:
Interpretive view of the Villa at its full extent.

main gate was the owner's winged-corridor house. Inside, the owner's wealth was displayed in fabulous mosaics showing animals, gods, heroes and strange creatures. To the north was an aisled farmhouse with many living rooms. To the south was a range of farm buildings.

Next to the main house was a pond set into the courtyard wall which may have been a garden feature. There were also two bath houses, one in the farmhouse and a bigger one to the south outside the courtyard.

Early Settlement and Development

Evidence from artefacts suggest that the site was occupied in the 1st century AD. Changes in building methods and materials in the main house also indicate that an earlier villa had existed. The aisled farmhouse too seems to have been altered over the years to create more living space. The range of farm buildings to the south may have been constructed as the agricultural output of the Villa grew and its prosperity increased.

In Roman times Bembridge harbour extended southwards as far as modern Sandown. Its easy access to sea transport may partly explain why Brading became the most successful villa on the Island.

The End of the Villa

Several pieces of evidence suggest a change in the fortunes of the villa in the 4th century AD. The large bath house was converted into an industrial building and part of the main house was turned over to farm activities. Inside a corn-drier was built into the corridor; animals were butchered in certain rooms; ploughs were stored there; and the mosaics were burnt. It would seem from the number of objects found there that the last occupants of the villa lived in the aisled farmhouse. But again we are left with an incomplete picture of the end of an Island villa.

Life at the Villas

Villa Owners

Roman Britons were people who lived in the province of Britannia, most of whom were descended from native ancestors. More is known about the owners than the other people who lived in villas.

At the start of the Romano-British period social class had more to do with ownership, but in time wealth became the important factor. From the evidence available it seems that most owners were of British stock. Some were ex-soldiers, officials, or landowners who lived in other provinces. Others may have been businessmen who lived in towns and had farm managers.

Daily Life

Villa owners would spend most of their time managing the estate and conducting business. Some also performed duties as local government officials. Their wives would have been busy too, running the house, and directing their servants. In wealthier homes children over seven would be educated by tutors.

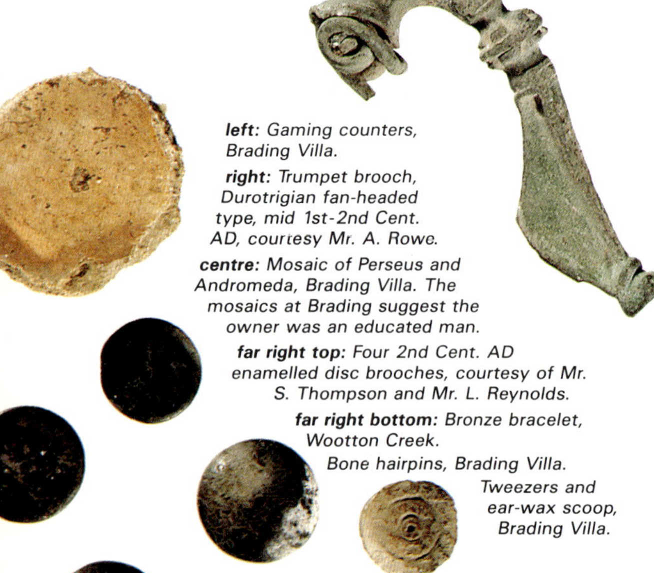

left: *Gaming counters, Brading Villa.*
right: *Trumpet brooch, Durotrigian fan-headed type, mid 1st-2nd Cent. AD, courtesy Mr. A. Rowe.*
centre: *Mosaic of Perseus and Andromeda, Brading Villa. The mosaics at Brading suggest the owner was an educated man.*
far right top: *Four 2nd Cent. AD enamelled disc brooches, courtesy of Mr. S. Thompson and Mr. L. Reynolds.*
far right bottom: *Bronze bracelet, Wootton Creek.*
Bone hairpins, Brading Villa.
Tweezers and ear-wax scoop, Brading Villa.

Dress

Our knowledge of the appearance of Romano-British people comes from a variety of sources including; wall paintings, mosaics and sculptures. Excavated textiles, leather and burials have also provided important information.

Equipment, such as tweezers and ear-wax scoops, have further shown that cleanliness

and grooming was an important aspect of appearance.

Materials used to make clothes included wool, linen and occasionally silk or cotton. Footwear consisted of leather shoes, boots or sandals.

Men wore their nightshirts as undergarments over which they would wear a coloured tunic. Togas were only worn on special occasions. For farmwork a tunic, trousers and boots was favoured. A *Byrrus Britannicus*, a long, hooded woollen cloak, might also have been worn. These became a famous export from Roman Britain.

Various cosmetics and perfumes were available for rich Romano-British women. Maids would dress their hair, which might have included hairpieces. Married women wore a dress called a *Stola* over their tunics. These came in many colours and designs.

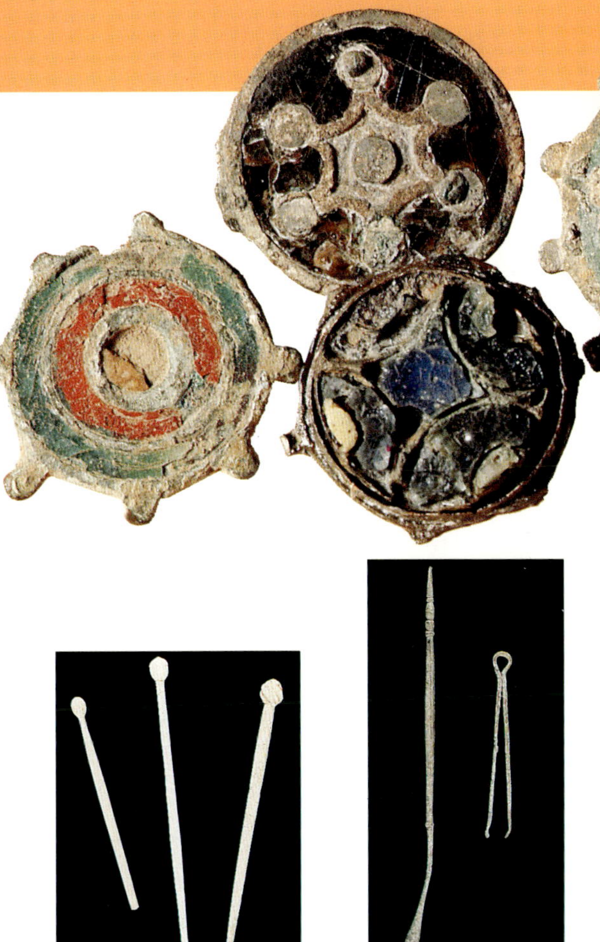

Shoes too were highly decorated. Shawls and wraps would have been worn outdoors. Jewellery completed a woman's outfit and included brooches, bracelets, ear-rings and necklaces.

Recreation

Life in Roman Britain was not all work. Marbles found at Newport, and counters for a board game at Brading, indicate time for recreation. The two most popular games in Roman Britain for which we have evidence were versions of backgammon and chess.

Among children's toys model dogs were popular. In Roman Britain there were many breeds of dog and at Brading the remains of two were found buried in a disused well. The wear patterns on their teeth suggest that they had been fed on lean meat and were probably, therefore, kept as pets. In contrast, the owner of Rock villa gave his dogs bones on which they could sharpen their teeth. Perhaps they were used for hunting, a suggestion supported by the large number of red deer bones and antler found at this site.

Life at the Villas

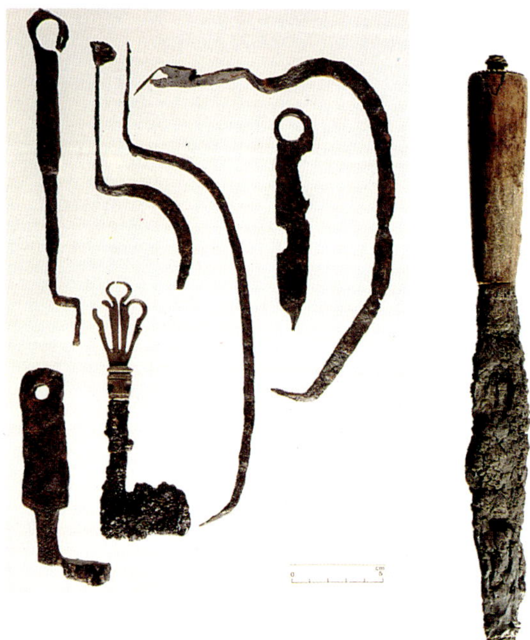

Inside the Villas

In the late Iron Age houses had one large space in which both cooking and sleeping, took place. Villa houses show that homes were now divided up into rooms for different uses. This seems to reflect a need for privacy arising from social changes.

Furnishing and Fittings

It is difficult to say how each room was used inside a villa. Few pieces of furniture or fittings have survived, but other evidence shows that rooms would have been furnished with chairs, couches, tables, wardrobes and shelves. The big key-plate from Brading shows that important doors had impressive metal fittings and complex locks. Various types of keys were used according to the level of security needed. At Brading iron fittings found in a doorway in the farmhouse give us some idea how doors worked. Light was provided by windows whose presence is often indicated by stone mouldings and the build-up of rubbish at points along the outside walls. Some windows were probably protected by wooden shutters and to keep out intruders the owner of Rock villa had metal grilles fitted. Extra light might have been provided by clay lamps, but they were used more widely as grave goods or religious offerings.

How the Rooms were used

Artefacts and features inside a room may sometimes give us clues about its uses. The large mosaic room at Brading for example probably served as both a sitting room and dining room.

Hypocaust was a luxury and is an indicator of the importance of the rooms. Fireplaces were popular features of Island villas and examples have been found at Combley, Carisbrooke and Newport. Perhaps real fires were chosen because they made rooms more attractive and cosy.

above left:

An assortment of keys and latch lifters from Brading Villa.

Bone handled knife, Rock Villa.

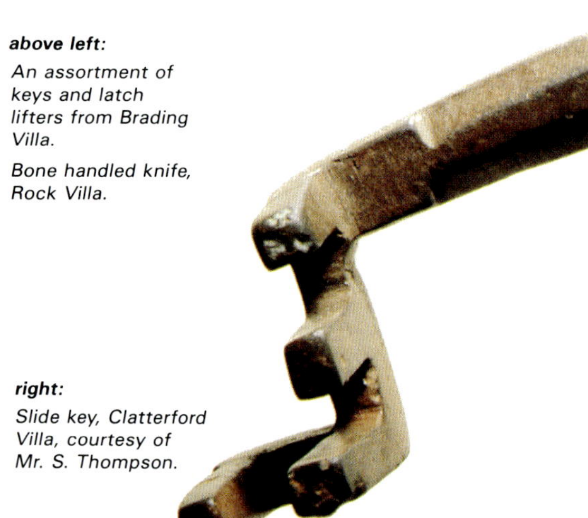

right:

Slide key, Clatterford Villa, courtesy of Mr. S. Thompson.

Bedrooms are difficult to identify because couches were often used as beds and so any living room could be slept in.

Kitchens are another problem because their

hearths and ovens rarely survive. Food was cooked in metal or pottery vessels placed on iron tripods or gridirons. These were put over hot charcoals spread on top of a raised hearth made of stone. Baking and roasting were done in ovens made of brick and rubble.

left:
Iron cooking tripod, Brading Villa.

above:
Pottery oil lamp 1st/2nd Cent AD, Gurnard Villa.

below: *Spoon bowls, Brading Villa.*
below right: *Mortaria mixing bowl, Brading Villa.*

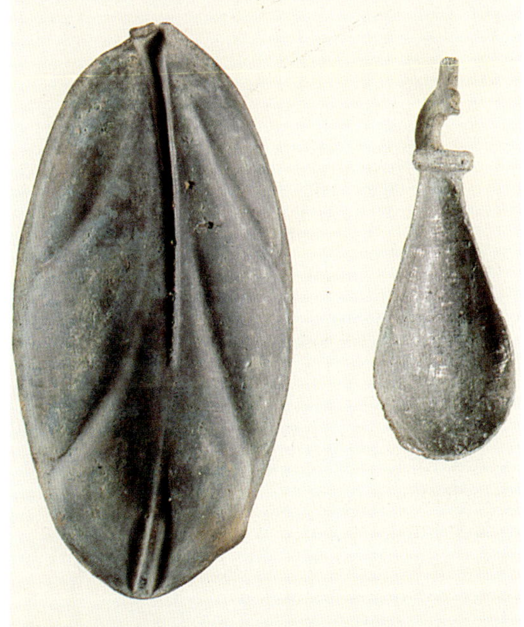

Food

The villa communities of the Island would have produced most of their own food. Stoneground flour was used daily for making bread, cake and pastries. Fruit and vegetables came from orchards and kitchen gardens. Bees were kept and their honey used as a sweetener. Salt was used for preserving and seasoning meat. Meat was plentiful, either from the farm, or from hunting and fishing trips. Oysters were very popular and large numbers of shells are found on all villa sites. On the Island they could easily be obtained from local beds around the Solent.

Baths and Bathing

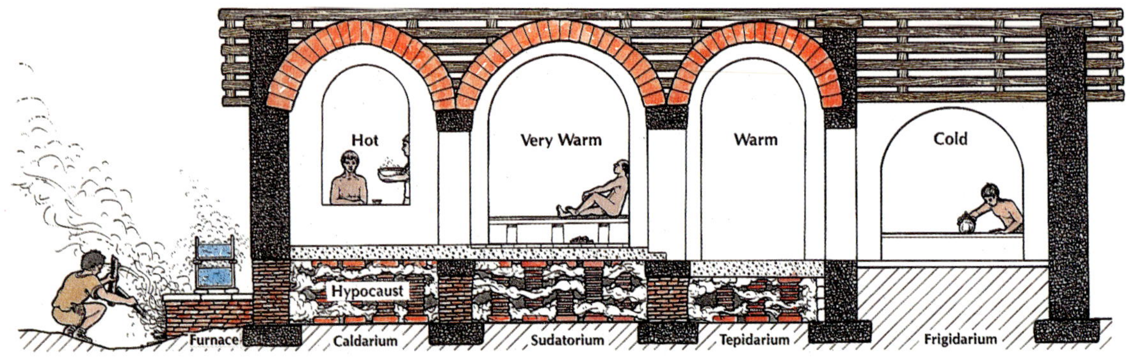

The Romans are famous for their public baths, and in the Romano-British countryside many rich villa owners had private baths built in their homes.

The Origin of Baths

Although the Greeks are thought to have invented baths it was the Romans who made them an important part of their daily lives. Their desire to bathe was linked to the days when Rome was an unhealthy place without sewers or clean water. To help change this situation fresh water was brought from the countryside into the city along specially built channels called *aqueducts*. Pipes then delivered the water into people's homes and into public buildings, such as the baths. The public baths were also places where people could relax, meet friends, swim, do business, play games and take some form of exercise.

Private Baths

Public baths could be found in the main towns of Roman Britain, but private baths were an important element of villas and on the Island the owners at Brading, Carisbrooke, Combley and Newport had them. They were all built in the same general style and may be seen as symbols of individual wealth and social status.

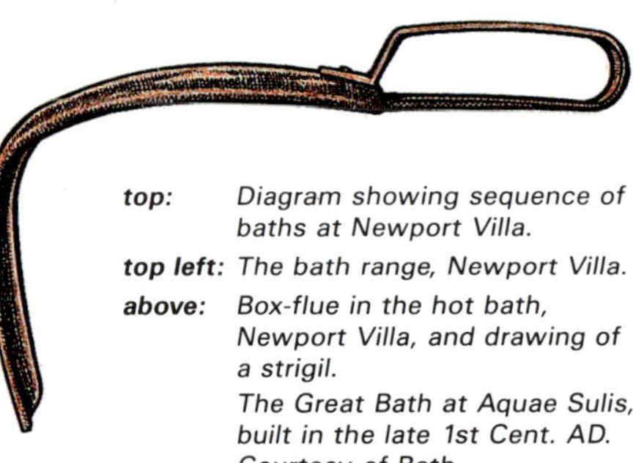

top: *Diagram showing sequence of baths at Newport Villa.*

top left: *The bath range, Newport Villa.*

above: *Box-flue in the hot bath, Newport Villa, and drawing of a strigil.*

The Great Bath at Aquae Sulis, built in the late 1st Cent. AD. Courtesy of Bath Archaeological Trust.

Hypocaust Heating

Baths and some living rooms were heated by the *hypocaust* system. This worked by means of a fire in a furnace which sent warm air under a room. In villas on the Island it was usual for the floor to be supported by brick pillars. The warm air circulated underneath and then up ducts made of hollow bricks set in the outside walls. These ducts had openings just below the edge of the roof and the cold air passing over them drew the warm air up. It is thought that hypocaust rooms were not heated all the time. Different forms of heating were used in the same house such as fireplaces and braziers.

Bathing

At Newport villa the method of bathing can be clearly seen. Bathers would change in the *apodyterium* and put on thick soled slippers.

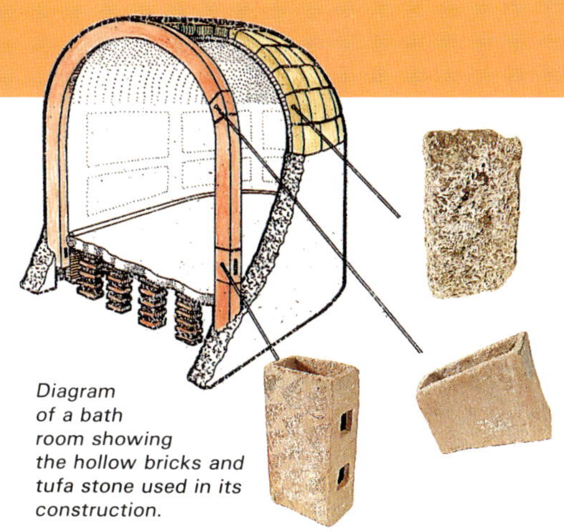

Diagram of a bath room showing the hollow bricks and tufa stone used in its construction.

Moving on to the hottest room, the *caldarium*, they would relax in the hot bath. The domed roof meant that condensation would run down the walls and not on the bathers head! In the drier atmosphere of the *sudatorium* they stretched out on benches. Fragrant oils were applied to their sweating bodies and scraped away with a *strigil*, a curved metal instrument. In the *frigidarium* bathers would take a cold plunge before drying themselves.

Farming

Agriculture in Roman Britain

After the Roman invasion farming continued much as before. Late Iron Age agricultural was very successful and surpluses were produced for export. Trends started in stock rearing and cereal storage continued.

The fertile soils of Southern England were intensively farmed during Roman times. Better ploughs enabled more areas to be cultivated. Fruit and vegetables were grown to supply the growing urban population. New types were introduced, such as carrots, celery, pears and plums. The introduction of the large scythe was important and led to an increase in hay meadows, animal feed and the numbers of livestock kept over winter.

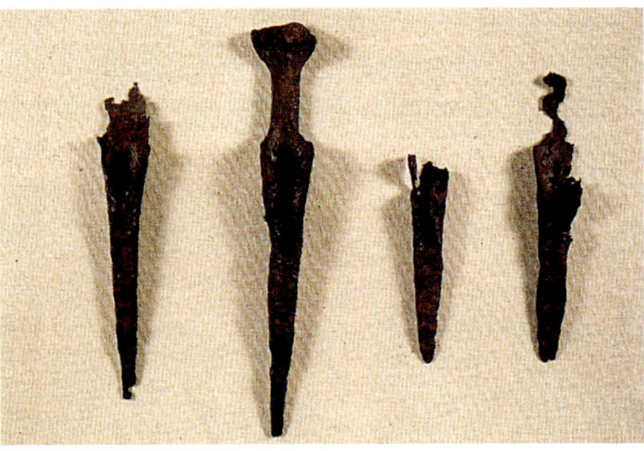

Cereal Farming

On Roman Wight fertile arable land and access to sea transport created the right conditions for profitable farming. The success of agriculture is shown by the growth of the villas. Most of them were situated along the central chalk downs enabling them to exploit the woodlands of the north, and fertile soils of the chalk and southern Greensand plain.

The main crops grown on the Island were wheat and barley. At Brading villa evidence shows that there were two types of plough which could be used to cultivate fields. The older method used ploughs called ards which grooved the soil. In the late Roman period new ploughs were introduced which cut and then turned the soil. Larger areas could now be cultivated and long fields were produced. Such fields have been identified on Brading Down

and probably belonged to the estate of the nearby villa. Crop rotation and manure spreading helped to keep the fields fertile.

After harvesting, the crops were taken to the villas for processing and storage in barns and granaries. In the 4th Century AD corn-drying kilns were introduced and four have been found on the Island. Apart from preparing corn for storage and milling it seems corn-driers might also have been used for ripening corn, drying pots and smoking food. At Rock and Brading they were built inside houses suggesting a dramatic change in the fortunes of these villas.

Antler horse harness fittings, Newport Villa.

Excavating Packway Corn-drier, Newchurch Farm 1983.

Livestock Farming

Sheep rearing was important in the late Iron Age, but evidence from the villas shows that it was less so in Roman times. Wool was still used locally for making clothes, as indicated by discoveries of spindle whorls and a bone weaving comb. The number of cattle and pigs kept on villas gradually increased during the Roman period. This was because they were good meat producers and fetched high prices at market. Other farm animals included chickens, geese, goats and oxen for ploughing. Some horses were kept too, perhaps for hunting, herding or for pulling carts and wagons.

Improvements to livestock farming were made during the Roman period through breeding, winter feeding and providing shelter. Growing fodder crops such as rape, vetch and turnip also meant that animals were better fed and improved soil fertility at the same time.

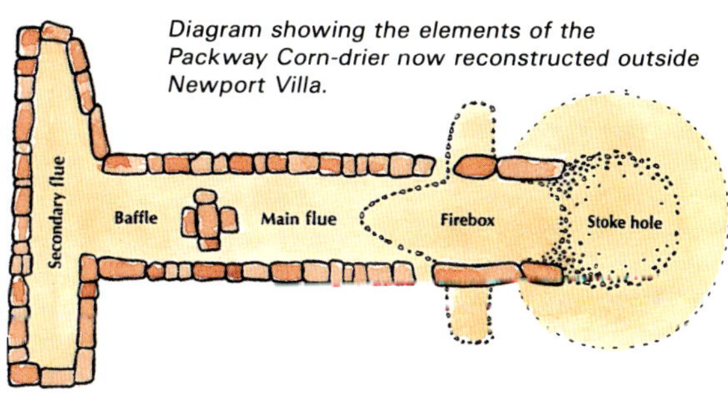

Diagram showing the elements of the Packway Corn-drier now reconstructed outside Newport Villa.

Agricultural production in Britain increased gradually during Roman times encouraged by a number of factors, such as the growth of towns and improvements in farming. The long period of peace during the 2nd and 3rd centuries AD, in contrast to the situation in the rest of the Western Empire, was equally important. It may explain why Roman Britain became so prosperous in the late 3rd century and why this was the main period of villa building in this country.

Bone weaving comb, Ventnor.

opposite:

Iron socks for the tips of wooden ard ploughs, Brading Villa.

Triptolemus the ploughman receiving corn from Ceres, Roman goddess of agriculture. Mosaic from Brading Villa.

This page above:

Iron share from a late Roman heavy plough. Brading Villa.

right:

Dorset shale spindle whorl, Clatterford Villa.

Crafts and Industries

The evidence of villa buildings, tools and fittings show that the Island community included skilled craftsmen.

Pottery

In the late Iron Age a pottery industry was started on the Island whose brown burnished products have been given the name Vectis Ware. The pottery forms copied those of the popular Black Burnished Ware from Poole. Vectis Ware was not as well made and served only local needs. Its production sites have not yet been positively identified, but Brading and Combley villas, as the largest sources of Vectis Ware, could well have been manufacturing centres. For unknown reasons Vectis Ware seems to have stopped being made in the early 4th century.

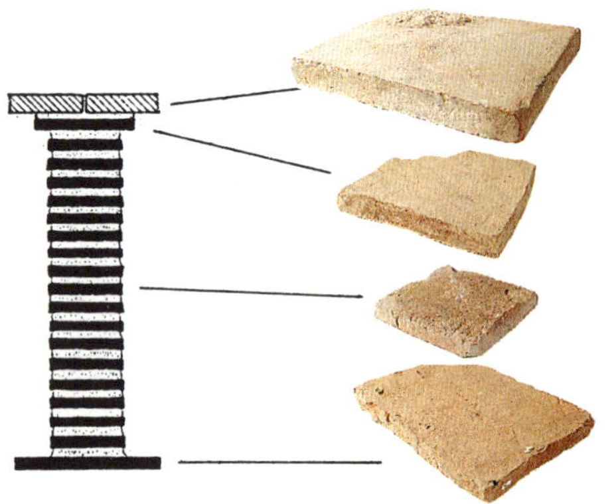

Brick and Tile

Clay roof tiles were used on most Island villas but especially at Combley. As a probable centre of the local pottery industry this villa may have also produced bricks and tiles. Elsewhere in Roman Britain there were large brickworks serving the needs of towns and the army.

Several different types of brick were made based on a standard size used throughout the Roman Empire. They were needed mainly for wall construction, hypocaust pillars and floors. Another form of brick used in hypocaust was the hollow box-flue type used to create heating ducts in the walls. Re-used brick and tile was also used in tessellated and mosaic floors.

Fingermarks of numerous different types have been found on many of the tiles and bricks. No-one is quite sure of their purpose, but they could be makers marks or counting devices. On box-flues comb patterns were made specifically to grip the mortar when they were set into the walls.

above left:
Neck of a Black Burnished Ware flagon, Wootton Creek.

below left:
A pila showing the different types of brick used.

below:
Various types of nails, Brading Villa.

above right:
Clay tile roofs used flat tegula tiles and curved imbrices nailed and mortared together.

Quarrying

Bembridge Limestone can only be found on the Isle of Wight, and outcrops occur on the beach and cliffs along the north east coast from Gurnard to Bembridge. It is a hard rock which can easily be worked and during the Roman period it was extensively used. A quern stone from South Hampshire shows that it was already being quarried and traded in the Iron Age. Quernstones of this material have also been found at Combley and Brading villas.

top: *Vectis Ware flagon in situ, Redcliff 1978.*
bottom: *The Flagon and other Vectis Ware from Redcliff.*

The first use of Bembridge Limestone after the Roman Conquest seems to be in the building of Fishbourne Palace around AD 70. Altars at Winchester and Dorchester, and a milestone found at Southampton show other ways in which it was used. During the late 3rd century AD blocks of Bembridge Limestone were used in the construction of the Roman fort at Porchester. It was also made into roof slabs for local building work.

The location of quarries on the Island in Roman times is uncertain. The unusual coastal location of Gurnard villa may indicate that it controlled the quarrying of Bembridge Limestone from nearby sources.

left: *Bembridge Limestone quern, Ventnor.*
below: *Bembridge Limestone on Gurnard beach.*

Salt Working

The inlets of the Solent provide ideal conditions for making salt. In Portsmouth harbour and Southampton Water salt was being processed from the late Iron Age onwards.

To make salt it was most important to have a long period of sunshine. The salt water was first collected in tanks and then boiled in simple clay vessels. These were then broken up to extract the salt cakes. The clay fragments are called *briquetage* and provide archaeologists with evidence of salt-making. Plant impressions on briquetage have also shown that it was a summer activity.

Salt-making sites of Roman date have been excavated at Wootton Creek and Yaverland. Briquetage has also been found at the late Iron Age site at Knighton, and the villas at Newport and Combley.

Trade

Britain became part of a common community with the Roman invasion. The Roman Empire was a kind of common market with vast communications and trading networks. The roads built by the army during the conquest later became the highways for transporting goods to the market towns and cities of Roman Britain and beyond. From Hadrian's Wall to the Nile in Egypt the Empire was connected by a system of trackways, roads, inns, canals, rivers and ports of trade. Route books, such as the early 2nd century AD Antonine Itinerary give us a picture of this system. Manufactured goods, foodstuffs and raw materials were bought and sold using a common coinage, under common laws and for common prices.

It was not only goods which were moved about, but people and ideas as well. The mosaics at Brading for example show design influences from the Continent, Italy and North Africa.

Boat hook, Brading Villa.

above: *Mosaic of a merman with steering oar and fruits of the sea, Brading Villa.*

'Astronomer' mosaic based on Italian wall paintings, Brading Villa.

Imported Goods

Our evidence for goods imported into the Isle of Wight comes mainly from stone, pottery and glass. At Bowcombe, a fragment of an engraved glass bowl was made in Egypt. Glass ware along with pottery beakers and a quernstone were all imports from the Rhineland found at Brading villa. Here too the marine mosaic panel and the presence of an

iron boat hook seem to emphasise the importance of the villa's location next to the largest natural harbour on the Island.

Evidence for local imports found in Island villas are supplied by quernstones made in Hertfordshire, Sussex and Surrey. Pottery came mainly from Dorset, the New Forest, North Hampshire and Oxford. Foreign pottery commonly found on Island villa sites include colour-coated vessels and glossy red Samian ware from Gaul. Large jars, called *amphorae,* from the Mediterranean containing wine, olives and fish sauce were also imported to the Island throughout the Roman period.

The Solent Trading Centre

The network of sheltered harbours of the Solent was given the name *'Magnus Portus'* by the second Century Roman geographer Ptolemy. Besides being a centre for the export of local goods to the rest of Roman Britain and Europe, the Solent was also the scene of local trade. Vectis Ware and Bembridge Limestone from the Island have been found in settlements

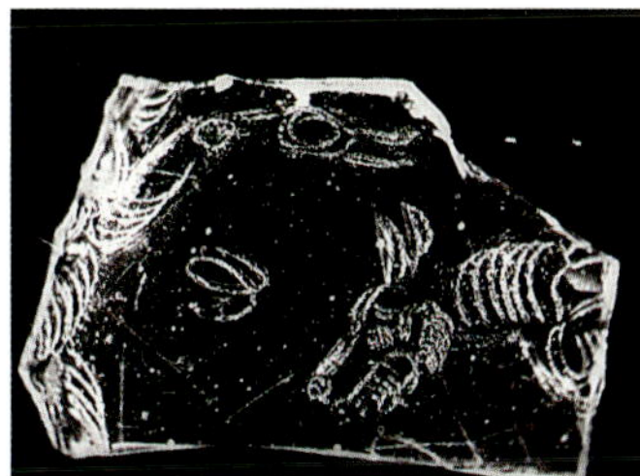

above:
Decorated Samian Ware bowl, Brading Villa.

right:
Amphora from the Solent.

top:
Engraved fragment of glass bowl made in Egypt, Bowcombe Villa.

above:
Anchor of Purbeck marble recovered from the seabed off Yarmouth.

along the mainland coast. Shale products from Dorset have also been found in Island villas including bracelets, dishes and spindle whorls.

Debris from Roman trading vessels is frequently dredged up around the Island's north coast by trawlers.

Recent work at Wootton Creek has revealed a beach site where trading took place. The salt-

right:
New Forest Ware products. Indented beakers from Newport and Carisbrooke Villas and a jug from Brading.

bottom:
Cow skull from Wootton Creek.

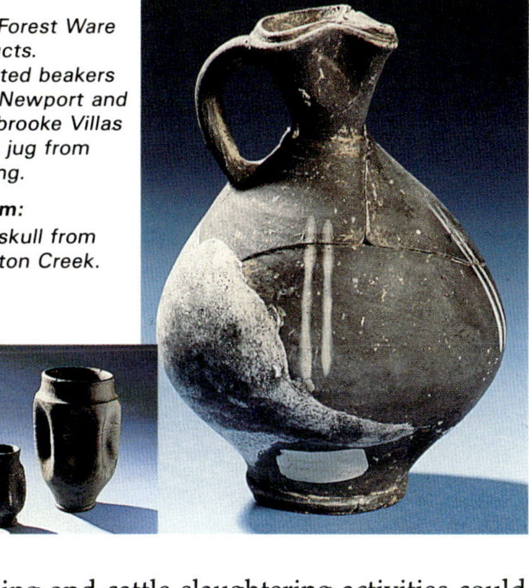

making and cattle slaughtering activities could also have been connected with supplying ships anchored in the Solent.

In medieval times the Solent was a gathering place for convoys of merchant ships and perhaps the same was true in Roman times. The suggestion is supported by a surviving historical account of AD 296 about the recapture of the breakaway province of Britannia. The document tells how the British commander, Allectus, used the sheltered havens of the Isle of Wight to gather his fleet to intercept the approaching Imperial task force. Unfortunately a sea fog ruined his plans and Roman Britain was returned to the Empire.

The End of Roman Britain

What Happened?

History books place the end of Roman Britain at AD 410, when the last known letter was sent from Rome to Britannia. In it the Emperor Honorius told the cities of the province to defend themselves. The message appears to be a reply to British concerns that the last regular Roman troops, which left in AD 407, had not returned. This had happened many times before but there now seems to have been greater anxiety. Ever since AD 367, when large raids in the north and west caused widespread destruction, Britannia had been under attack. Along the south and east coasts the raiders included Angles, Saxons, Franks and Jutes.

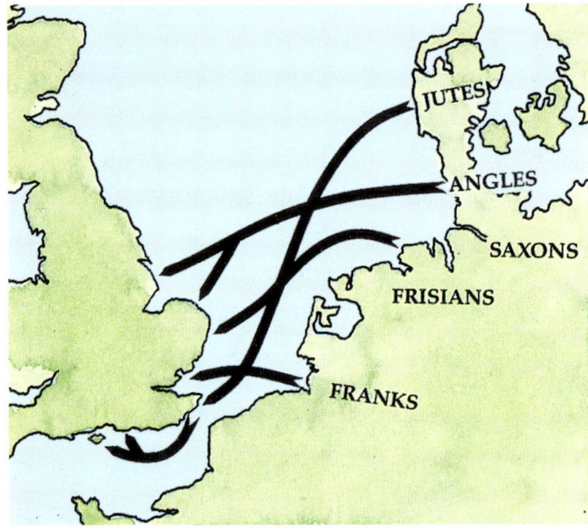

Roman Britain had been changing long before AD 410, and some scholars believe that the country had in fact ceased to be 'Roman' by the end of the 4th century. The reasons why this happened are complex, but the result was the collapse of an economic system involving the inter-play between the army, taxes, towns and agriculture.

In Roman Britain more and more troops were taken away to support revolts, or to defend Rome. During the same period the economy and way of life gradually changed, and standards of living declined. The end of Roman Britain was one of gradual change to meet the demands of new circumstances.

The End of the Villas

Archaeological evidence indicates a fairly rapid decline in the fortunes of the Island's villas during the early 4th century. By the middle of the century they all seem to be in decay. Why this happened and when they were each finally abandoned is uncertain. There may have been several reasons, such as the fear of raiders, business failure, or because more powerful landowners took them over.

***above*:** *Roman hound brooch found in Anglo-Saxon grave, Bowcombe Down.*

far left: Map showing the invasions and migrations of Germanic peoples into Britain 4th-6th Centuries.

below left: *A pair of silver gilt and garnet brooches, mid-6th Cent. AD, from Shalcombe Down and a quoit brooch from Clatterford Villa, 5th Cent. AD, courtesy of Mr. S. Thompson.*

above: *Shield boss and spearhead. Amber glass bracelet and pin from the Down Anglo-Saxon Cemeteries.*

Page from Rev. J. Skinner's notebook of excavations on Chessell Down 1816-1818.

right: *Silver sceat. Early 8th Cent. AD. Found near Carisbrooke Castle. Courtesy of Mr. S. Thompson. Anglo-Saxon Warrier.*

The Coming of the Jutes

In the year AD 449 the Anglo-Saxon Chronicle reads: "From the Jutes came the people of Kent and the people of the Isle of Wight ..."

Recent studies suggest that the Isle of Wight was settled by Jutes from Kent in the late 5th or early 6th century AD. This event appears to form part of the wider conquest of South Wessex led by Cerdic and Cynric, who gave the Island to their nephews, Stuf and Whitgar.

Place-names have been used to detect early Anglo-Saxon settlements on the Isle of Wight. They show that most people were living in the south, as in Roman times, with a more populated area along the East Yar valley. Archaeological discoveries also suggest that there were important settlements in the west.

The evidence comes from 19th century excavations of two large cemeteries on Bowcombe and Chessell Downs. The grave goods show us that they were Jutish people from Kent and the finds have dated the cemeteries to the early 6th century AD. Some of the objects from Chessell may be seen in the British Museum.

During the 1970's another rich cemetery of early 6th century AD date was excavated in Carisbrooke Castle. In late Anglo-Saxon times it became a fortified site overlooking the Bowcombe valley, where recent finds have hinted at the presence of other Anglo-Saxon settlements.

Current work on Roman Wight

At present the Unit does not carry out many excavations. It is however engaged in a government backed project involving special fieldwork. This is taking place around Wootton Creek where prehistoric, Roman and Medieval discoveries have been made. In Roman times the Creek appears to have been used as a haven where goods were brought ashore, and Island products were exchanged. Part of future work will look at the off-shore shoals in the Solent, where there are indications that Roman galleys may have anchored.

What We Would Like to Know

There are many areas for future archaeological research. In some ways we know very little about Roman times on the Isle of Wight. Most of our evidence comes from villas where the wealthiest people lived. What about the rest of the Island's population – where did they live? What sort of settlements did they have? Where were the pottery kilns making Vectis Ware? Where was Bembridge Limestone quarried? These and other questions will only be answered by new discoveries being reported, and by more fieldwork.

left: *Taking samples of wood from Wootton Creek for Carbon 14 dating.*

below left: *Glass cup of late Roman date. Wootton Creek.*

below: *Gold Solidus of Valentinian II, AD 383-392, from Thorness Beach recently acquired for the Isle of Wight County Archaeological Collection.*

What to do if you find something.

People often discover objects whilst going about their everyday work, or for walks in the countryside. Although you may think your find is rubbish it could be valuable archaeological evidence for an area. For this reason it is important that you report your find to your local Museum or County Archaeologist. They will be happy to identify your object and advise you how to care for it.

When you find something, record how and where you made your discovery. Try to make a sketch of the findspot and mark it on a map. In this way you will be helping to preserve important archaeological information.